THIS LAND IS YOUR LAND

Georgia

BY ANN HEINRICHS

Content Adviser: Roger Smith, Director of Education and Outreach, The Georgia Historical Society, Savannah, Georgia

Reading Adviser: Dr. Linda D. Labbo, Department of Reading Education, College of Education, The University of Georgia

COMPASS POINT BOOKS MINNEAPOLIS, MINNESOTA

Compass Point Books
3109 West 50th Street, #115
Minneapolis, MN 55410

Visit Compass Point Books on the Internet at *www.compasspointbooks.com*
or e-mail your request to *custserv@compasspointbooks.com*

On the cover: Red fields on a Georgia farm

Photographs ©: Kevin Fleming/Corbis, cover, 1, 21; TRIP, 3, 6, 12, 14, 30, 35, 45; Georgia Department of Industry, Trade, & Tourism, 5, 7, 8, 10, 13, 15, 24, 27, 28, 38, 40, 41, 42, 43 (top), 44 (middle), 47; David Muench/Corbis, 9; Topham, 16, 22, 31, 32, 33, 37; Corbis, 17; Medford Historical Collection/Corbis, 18; Georgia Historical Society, 19; NARA, 20, 46; W. Cody/Corbis, 25; Owaki-Kulla/Corbis, 26; CNN/Getty Images, 29; Getty Images News & Sport, 34, 48 (top); William A. Bake/Corbis, 39; Robesus, Inc, 43 (state flag); One Mile Up, Inc., 43 (state seal); PhotoDisc, 44 (top); Comstock, 44 (bottom).

Editors: E. Russell Primm, Emily J. Dolbear, and Catherine Neitge
Photo Researchers: Svetlana Zhurkina and Image Select International
Photo Selector: Linda S. Koutris
Designer/Page Production: The Design Lab/Jaime Martens
Cartographer: XNR Productions, Inc.

Library of Congress Cataloging-in-Publication Data
Heinrichs, Ann.
  Georgia / by Ann Heinrichs.
      v. cm. — (This land is your land)
Includes bibliographical references and index.
Contents: Welcome to Georgia!—Mountains, valleys, and plains—A trip through time—Government by the people—Georgians at work—Getting to know Georgians—Let's explore Georgia!—Important dates.
  ISBN 0-7565-0321-3 (hardcover)
  1. Georgia—Juvenile literature. [1. Georgia.] I. Title.
  F286.3 .H45 2003
  975.8—dc21   2002010055

Table of Contents

NOTE: In this book, words that are defined in the glossary are in **bold** the first time they appear in the text.

William Bartram was a scientist who studied plants. He traveled through Georgia in 1773. There he found wild forests and fertile plains. He admired Georgia's large, healthy peach trees. He also loved Georgia's sweet-smelling pine trees.

Many things about Georgia are still the same. Its soil is rich and fertile. Georgia grows more peanuts than any other state. Georgia's juicy peaches are now the state fruit. Georgia is also famous for its pine forests.

Atlanta, Georgia's capital city, was burned in 1864 during the Civil War (1861–1865). Today, Atlanta is a big, busy city. Some people call Atlanta the capital of the South.

Georgians are proud of their modern factories. They are equally proud of their land and **wildlife.** Now come and discover Georgia for yourself. It's a great place to explore!

▲ **Stone Mountain is the largest granite outcropping on Earth. It features a huge sculpture of Confederate leaders.**

▲ A shrimp boat on the Savannah River

Georgia is the largest state in the South. It is also the largest state east of the Mississippi River. On the southeast, Georgia touches the Atlantic Ocean. The Savannah River empties into the ocean. This river forms most of Georgia's eastern border. Just across the river is South Carolina.

Tennessee and North Carolina are Georgia's northern neighbors. Florida lies along the southern border. Georgia and Florida share the Okefenokee Swamp. The Chattahoochee River forms much of Georgia's western border. Alabama lies on the other side.

▲ **Canoeing on Georgia's Okefenokee Swamp**

▲ **Brasstown Bald Mountain in the Appalachians**

The Appalachian Mountains cover northern Georgia. This is a region of mountains, valleys, and rocky hills. Northeastern Georgia is the Blue Ridge section of the Appalachians. Georgia's highest peak—Brasstown Bald Mountain—rises here.

Many rivers cut through Georgia's northern mountains. One river forms Amicalola Falls, Georgia's highest waterfall. Amicalola means "tumbling water" in the Cherokee language. The rich farmland of the northern river valleys provides good grazing land for cattle.

▲ **Scenic Amicalola Falls in Georgia's northern mountains**

Dams have been built on many northern rivers to hold back water. They also create huge lakes, including Lake Sidney Lanier and Allatoona Lake.

The Piedmont **Plateau** lies south of the Appalachians. Its rolling hills slope gently toward the south. Atlanta, the state capital, sits on this plateau.

▲ **A road passes over Allatoona Lake.**

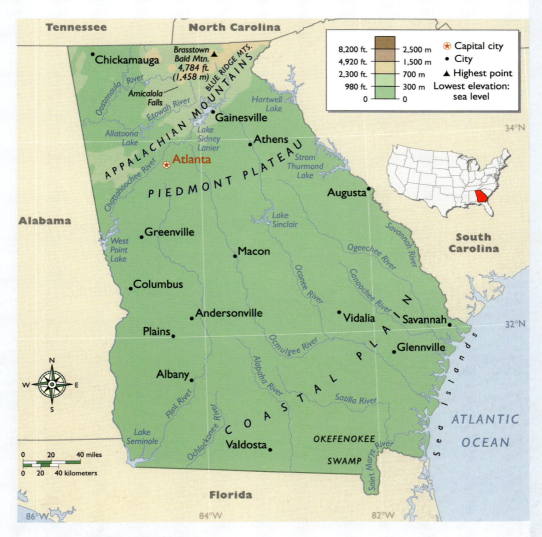

▲ A topographic map of Georgia

Low plains cover the southern half of Georgia. Farmers there grow peanuts, cotton, and other crops. Much of Georgia's seacoast is marshy, or wet. Its long grasses, called sea oats,

▲ Savannah's City Hall

help keep the sand in place. Savannah is the most important city along the coast.

South of Savannah and just off the coast are Georgia's Sea Islands. Most of these islands remain in a natural and wild state. They are covered with forests, **sand dunes,** and **marshes.** Crabs and sea turtles thrive there.

Forests cover more than half of Georgia. Deer, raccoons, opossums, rabbits, and foxes live in these wooded areas. Alligators, bears, and wildcats lurk in the Okefenokee Swamp.

Many waterbirds live along its shores. Strange plants called Spanish moss hang from the trees.

Georgia is warm and sunny in summer. Winters don't get

▲ **Wildflowers bloom on one of Georgia's Sea Islands.**

▲ A fountain in Savannah's Forsythe Park

very cold, except in the far north. People in snowy states might like Georgia's winters. Georgia averages only about 1 inch (2.5 centimeters) of snow a year!

Many people lived in Georgia two thousand years ago. They were called the Mound Builders because they built huge mounds, or piles of earth and stones. Some mounds were used as graves. Others were used for religious ceremonies. Many of these mounds still stand today.

▲ **Indian mounds still exist at Etowah Indian Mounds State Historic Site in Cartersville.**

▲ **General James Oglethorpe was the founder of Savannah.**

Later, the Creek Indians settled in Georgia. They lived on the southern plains. The Creeks lived in huts with wooden or grass roofs. Each town had an open space in the center where the people held dances, meetings, and religious festivals.

The Cherokee Indians lived in the northern river valleys. Cherokee villages had many dome-shaped houses. The people held meetings in large council houses. Timucua, Yamassee, and other Indian groups lived in Georgia, too.

The Spanish explorer Hernando de Soto passed through this area in 1540. He found many great kingdoms among the native people. Later, Great Britain set up **colonies** in North America. James Oglethorpe started the colony of Georgia. In 1733, Oglethorpe founded what is now Savannah. That was Georgia's first European **settlement.**

Soon Georgia and the other colonies wanted their freedom. They fought the Revolutionary War (1775–1783)—and won! In 1788, Georgia became the fourth U.S. state by **ratifying** the Constitution.

Many new settlers came to farm Georgia's rich soil. Some farmers grew cotton on huge farms called plantations. Slavery was made legal in Georgia in 1749. The plantation owners forced people from Africa to work as slaves. Little by little, the

▲ African slaves were forced to work on Georgia's plantations.

▲ **Union General William Tecumseh Sherman destroyed Atlanta but let Savannah stand.**

Creek people gave up their land. In the 1830s, the Cherokee, too, were forced to leave.

Meanwhile, Northern and Southern states argued about slavery. Georgia and other Southern states finally broke away from the Union. They formed the Confederate States of America. Soon the Civil War began. Many bloody battles took place in Georgia. In the Battle of Chickamauga, for example, thousands of soldiers were killed or wounded. In 1864, General William Tecumseh Sherman of the Union army marched through Georgia. He destroyed Atlanta in his march toward the sea, but he spared Savannah. In 1864, he gave the city to President Abraham Lincoln as a Christmas gift!

After the Civil War, many busy factories started up in Georgia. Farmers began to raise much more than just cotton. They grew corn, fruit, tobacco, and many other crops. Georgia's farm and factory goods were useful during World War II (1939–1945).

▲ Georgia's lumber industry was useful during World War II.

In the 1960s, African-Americans struggled to gain equal rights. Dr. Martin Luther King Jr. led the way. He was a minister from Atlanta.

Today, Georgia works hard to protect its land and wildlife. Good highways make it easier for people to travel there. They discover a land of great natural beauty.

▲ **Dr. Martin Luther King Jr. leading a civil rights march in Washington, D.C.**

▲ **Some of Georgia's many busy highways**

Government by the People

▲ **Georgia native Jimmy Carter was president from 1977 to 1981 and winner of the 2002 Nobel Peace Prize.**

Georgia is proud of its leaders. They have made a big difference in the world. Jimmy Carter was America's thirty-ninth president. Dr. Martin Luther King Jr. was a great civil rights leader. Clarence Thomas became a judge on the U.S. Supreme Court. Andrew Young was the U.S. **ambassador** to the United Nations. All these leaders began their work in Georgia.

Like the U.S. government, Georgia's state government has three branches—legislative, executive, and judicial. The three branches keep a check on one another. They make sure that no branch gets too powerful.

Tennessee

North Carolina

South Carolina

Alabama

Florida

ATLANTIC OCEAN

- Chickamauga
- Gainesville
- Athens
- Atlanta
- Augusta
- Greenville
- Macon
- Columbus
- Andersonville
- Vidalia
- Savannah
- Plains
- Glennville
- Albany
- Valdosta

Oostanaula River
Etowah River
Hartwell Lake
Allatoona Lake
Lake Sidney Lanier
Chattahoochee River
Strom Thurmond Lake
Lake Sinclair
West Point Lake
Oconee River
Ogeechee River
Canoochee River
Savannah River
Ocmulgee River
Alapaha River
Satilla River
Flint River
Lake Seminole
Ochlockonee River
Saint Marys River

Capital city
City

34°N
32°N

N
W   E
S

0   20   40 miles
0   20   40 kilometers

86°W   84°W   82°W

▲ A geopolitical map of Georgia

The legislative branch makes the state laws. Georgia's lawmakers serve in the general assembly. It has two houses, or parts. One is the 56-member senate. The other is the 180-member house of representatives.

The executive branch makes sure the state's laws are obeyed. Georgia's governor leads the executive branch. Voters elect the governor to a four-year term. The governor chooses people to help him in many executive jobs. The voters elect some important state officers, too. Two of these are the lieutenant governor and the secretary of state.

Georgia's judges and courts make up the judicial branch. Judges decide whether someone has broken the law. Georgia's highest court is the state supreme court. Voters elect its seven judges.

Georgia is divided into 159 counties. Most are governed by a board of commissioners. Two counties—Union and Towns—are governed by judges. Cities, towns, and villages may elect governments, too. Most have a mayor, or manager, and a city council.

▲ **The Walton County Courthouse in Monroe**

▲ Georgia's capitol in Atlanta.

Did you ever bite into an onion? Maybe you'd rather not! You might enjoy biting into one of Georgia's Vidalia onions, though. People chomp into them as if they were apples!

Vidalia onions are one of nature's mysteries. Georgia farmers raise them around Vidalia and Glennville. Onions grown there taste sweet. Onions grown anywhere else taste hot!

▲ **Vidalia onions are a Georgia specialty.**

▲ **This machine is used to harvest peanuts in Georgia.**

Besides its onions, Georgia is famous for its three Ps—peanuts, pecans, and peaches. Georgia is the leading state for peanuts and pecans. Peanuts are sometimes called "goobers." So, Georgia is often called the Goober State. The Peach State is another name for Georgia. Peaches from Georgia are tasty and healthful.

Georgia is also first in broilers, or young chickens. They are the state's most valuable farm product. Georgians also produce cotton, tomatoes, and eggs.

▲ A worker concentrates on the details of making carpet.

Many Georgia farm products go to food factories. In fact, foods are Georgia's leading factory products. They include bakery goods, peanut butter, and soft drinks.

Textiles are the state's second-biggest factory product. Georgia's most important textile is carpet material. The carpet industry is centered in Dalton in extreme northwest Georgia. Only North Carolina makes more carpeting. Georgia's factories also make cars, airplane parts, and chemicals.

So far, we've looked at products that Georgia sells. Most Georgia workers sell services, however. Teachers, nurses, and airplane pilots are service workers. So are news reporters. Hundreds of reporters work for Cable News Network (CNN), based in Atlanta. Tourism is also an important industry, especially in Atlanta and Savannah. Clearly, service workers have special skills. They use these skills to help others.

▲ The news station CNN is based in Atlanta.

▲ Atlanta is Georgia's biggest city.

In 2000, more than 8 million people lived in Georgia. That made it tenth in population among the states. Georgia had gained almost 2 million people since 1990!

Before 1960, most Georgians lived in rural areas. Those are areas outside of cities and towns. Today, about half of all Georgians live near Atlanta. The next-largest cities are Augusta, Columbus, and Savannah.

Georgia's first European settlers were English people. They lived mainly along the coast, and many of their **descendants** still live in Georgia. Spanish, Portuguese, German, and Jewish settlers arrived later. Other settlers came from Austria and Switzerland. Scottish and Irish people came from nearby states. Almost three of every ten Georgians are African-Americans.

▲ A father and son fish off the bank of Sweetwater Creek Lake.

▲ Julia Roberts, a famous Hollywood
movie star, is from Georgia

Some have descended from former slaves. Many moved into Georgia later to work. Other Georgians have Asian, Hispanic, or Native American roots.

Many famous music stars came from Georgia. For example, Little Richard, James Brown, and Otis Redding were all born in Macon. Ray Charles is another Georgia musician. Actors Laurence Fishburne III, Julia Roberts, Holly Hunter, and Joanne Woodward are Georgians, too.

Georgia writers are widely known and loved. Alice Walker is best known for *The Color Purple* (1982). Joel Chandler

Harris wrote the "Uncle Remus" stories based on African-American folktales.

Margaret Mitchell wrote *Gone with the Wind* (1936). It shows Southern life in Civil War times. Another world-famous Georgia writer is Flannery O'Connor. She won the 1972 National Book Award for fiction.

Georgia has produced many sports stars, too. Jackie Robinson was the first African-American in major-league baseball. Hank Aaron was a batting champion whose 755 home runs set an all-time record. World-famous golf stars show up in Augusta every April. They compete in the Masters golf tournament.

▲ Margaret Mitchell's *Gone with the Wind* won the 1937 Pulitzer Prize.

Atlanta's sports events are often in the news. Atlanta proudly hosted the 1996 Olympic Games. Football's Super Bowl was held in Atlanta twice. Five of baseball's World Series games were held there, too. Atlanta is also home to Georgia's professional sports teams. Baseball fans cheer for the Atlanta Braves. Football fans have the Atlanta Falcons. The Atlanta Hawks are Georgia's basketball stars.

▲ In 1996 the Olympic Games came to Atlanta. The flame blazed atop the Olympic Stadium.

▲ **Nearly thirteen thousand Union soldiers are buried in the Andersonville National Cemetery.**

Crouch down in the Chickamauga battlefield. You can imagine how hard it was to fight there. The trees and bushes are very thick. An important Civil War battle took place at Chickamauga, but the soldiers could hardly see one another. Thousands of people were killed in this dreadful battle.

Andersonville is another famous Civil War site. It was once a prison camp for Union soldiers. Today, the National

▲ Places to visit in Georgia

Prisoner of War Museum is there. It honors all U.S. prisoners of war. Columbus, Georgia, is home to the Port Columbus National Civil War Naval Museum.

Many old houses stand in Savannah's historic district. Some

streets are made of tabby. This is a white concrete made with oyster shells. Savannah's 2.5-square-mile (4-square-kilometer) National Historic Landmark District is America's largest historic district. Savannah's Victorian District is rich in black history. Its First African Baptist Church is the oldest black church in North America. In the Second African Baptist Church, Savannah's slaves first got the news that they were free.

▲ **Savannah has many beautiful old homes.**

▲ **Martin Luther King Jr. was born in this house in Atlanta.**

In the state capitol in Atlanta, you can watch state lawmakers at work. The capitol is also a museum. It displays historic flags and Native American objects. Today, people can visit the birthplace, church, and grave of Martin Luther King Jr., who lived in Atlanta. They're all part of a national historic site.

A woodworker makes a stool from a tree. A potter molds wet clay into a pitcher. Sparks fly as a blacksmith hammers hot metal. These are some of the sights you'll see in Westville. It's a living-history village. Here, people live as Georgians in the 1850s.

Try to imagine a "music factory." You could play any instrument there. You could write a new tune. You could play a giant keyboard by walking on the keys! You can do all these things at the Music Factory. It's in Macon's Georgia Music Hall of Fame.

Ocmulgee National Monument stands near Macon. Long ago, Native Americans built huge mounds there. Visitors can also explore the underground room where Native Americans held religious meetings.

▲ **The mounds at Ocmulgee National Monument**

Pirates used to hide on Georgia's Sea Islands. Today, many of the islands are protected places. Plants and animals there are kept safe from harm. Huge sea turtles lay eggs on the islands. When the baby turtles hatch, they run to the sea.

The Okefenokee Swamp is another wildlife area. Long-legged birds go fishing along the banks. They grab the fish with their long bills. You may see raccoons, bears, or even wildcats, but you will surely see alligators. They all make Georgia a great place to explore!

▲ Live oak trees covered in Spanish moss are a common sight in Georgia.

Important Dates

1540 Hernando de Soto passes through what is now Georgia.

1732 The Georgia colony is established by a charter granted by King George II of England.

1733 The first British settlers arrive.

1778 Savannah is captured in the Revolutionary War.

1788 Georgia becomes the fourth U.S. state on January 2.

1838 The last of the Cherokee people leave Georgia.

1861 Georgia leaves the Union and joins the Confederacy.

1863 Confederates win the Battle of Chickamauga in the Civil War.

1864 Union General William T. Sherman burns Atlanta and begins the March to the Sea.

1870 Georgia rejoins the Union.

1912 Juliette Gordon Low founds the Girl Scouts of America in Savannah.

1943 Georgia is the first state where eighteen-year-olds can vote.

1977 Georgia's Jimmy Carter becomes president of the United States.

1988 Georgia suffers a serious drought.

1994 Floods in central and southern Georgia cause terrible damage.

1996 The Summer Olympic Games are held in Georgia.

2002 Former president Jimmy Carter wins the Nobel Peace Prize.

Glossary

ambassador—a person who represents his or her country in another country

colonies—territories that belong to the country that settles them

descendants—a person's children, grandchildren, great-grandchildren, and their offspring

marshes—wetlands

plateau—high, flat land

ratifying—formally approving

sand dunes—hills of sand created by wind and water

settlement—a new town or village

wildlife—wild animals and plants

Did You Know?

★ The *Cherokee Phoenix,* the first newspaper in a Native American language, was published in New Echota in 1828. Articles appeared in both the English and Cherokee alphabet.

★ Six Flags Over Georgia is a theme park in Atlanta. It is named for the six flags that flew over Georgia. They are the flags of England and Spain, as well as the Liberty, Georgia, Confederate, and United States flags.

★ The Okefenokee Swamp's name comes from a Native American word. *Okefenokee* means "trembling earth."

★ Georgia is named after Great Britain's King George II.

★ Former U.S. president Jimmy Carter was born and grew up in Plains.

★ Savannah's First African Baptist Church was founded in 1773. The diamond-shaped holes in its floor enabled runaway slaves hiding downstairs to breathe.

★ John Pemberton of Atlanta invented Coca-Cola in 1886. He called it a "brain and nerve tonic." Today, the Coca-Cola Company is based in Atlanta.

State capital: Atlanta

State motto: Wisdom, Justice, and Moderation

State nicknames: Empire State of the South, Peach State, Cracker State, Goober State

Statehood: January 2, 1788; fourth state

Area: 58,930 square miles (152,627 sq km); **rank:** twenty-first

Highest point: Brasstown Bald Mountain, 4,784 feet (1,458 m) above sea level

Lowest point: Sea level, along the Atlantic coast

Highest recorded temperature: 112°F (44°C) at Greenville on August 20, 1983

Lowest recorded temperature: −17°F (−27°C) in Floyd County on January 27, 1940

Average January temperature: 47°F (8°C)

Average July temperature: 80°F (27°C)

Population in 2000: 8,186,453; **rank:** tenth

Largest cities in 2000: Atlanta (416,474), Augusta (199,775), Columbus (186,291), Savannah (131,510)

Factory products: Food products, transportation equipment, chemicals

Farm products: Chickens, peanuts, cotton, eggs

Mining products: Clay, crushed stone

State flag: Georgia's state flag shows the state seal against a field of blue. Thirteen white stars surround the seal. Beneath it is a gold banner. It has small images of three previous Georgia state flags, with American flags on each side. Under the banner are the words "In God We Trust."

State seal: Georgia's state seal shows three pillars. They stand for the three branches of state government. The pillars support an arch that says "Constitution." A man with a sword stands under the arch. He is defending the constitution. A banner weaves through the pillars. On it is the state motto. At the bottom is 1776, the date of the Declaration of Independence. The back of the seal shows symbols of Georgia's trade and agriculture. They are a ship with cotton and tobacco and a man plowing.

State abbreviations: Ga. (traditional); GA (postal)

State Symbols

State bird: Brown thrasher

State game bird: Bobwhite quail

State flower: Cherokee rose

State wildflower: Azalea

State tree: Live oak

State fruit: Peach

State fish: Largemouth bass

State marine mammal: Right whale

State reptile: Gopher tortoise

State possum: Pogo possum

State insect: Honeybee

State butterfly: Tiger swallowtail

State mineral: Staurolite

State seashell: Knobbed whelk

State gem: Quartz

State crop: Peanut

State vegetable: Vidalia sweet onion

State fossil: Shark tooth

State commemorative quarter:
Released on July 19, 1999

Making Georgia Peach Cobbler

Peaches are Georgia's favorite fruit!

Makes 12 servings.

INGREDIENTS:

½ cup butter or margarine

1 cup flour

1 cup sugar

1 teaspoon baking powder

1 cup milk

1 large can peaches, sliced or halved

DIRECTIONS:

Make sure an adult helps when you use the oven. Preheat the oven to 350°F. While the oven is heating up, cut up the butter or margarine. Put the pieces in a 9- by 13-inch pan. Set the butter in the oven to melt, but don't let it get bubbling hot. Mix the flour, sugar, and baking powder together. Stir in the milk and mix well. Pour this mixture into the pan of melted butter. Do not stir! Spread the peaches evenly across the top. Bake 50 to 60 minutes, until golden brown.

"Georgia on My Mind"

Words by Stuart Gorrell, music by Hoagy Carmichael

Melodies bring memories
That linger in my heart
Make me think of Georgia
Why did we ever part?

Some sweet day when blossoms fall
And all the world's a song
I'll go back to Georgia
'Cause that's where I belong.

Georgia, Georgia, the whole day through
Just an old sweet song keeps Georgia on my mind.
Georgia, Georgia, a song of you
Comes as sweet and clear as moonlight through the pines.

Other arms reach out to me
Other eyes smile tenderly
Still in peaceful dreams I see
The road leads back to you.

Georgia, Georgia, no peace I find
Just an old sweet song keeps Georgia on my mind.

James Brown (1933–) is a rhythm-and-blues singer. He's called the "Godfather of Soul."

Jimmy Carter (1924–) was the thirty-ninth U.S. president (1977–1981). He also served as governor of Georgia (1971–1975) and won the 2002 Nobel Peace Prize.

Ray Charles (1930–) is a blues and jazz singer, pianist, and composer. He lost his sight at age seven.

Laurence Fishburne III (1961–) is an actor. His movies include *Boyz N the Hood* (1991), *Apocalypse Now* (1979), and *The Matrix* (1999).

Joel Chandler Harris (1848–1908) was a writer of Southern folklore. He wrote the "Uncle Remus" tales.

Martin Luther King Jr. (1929–1968) was a civil rights leader. He helped get the Civil Rights Act of 1964 passed. King (pictured above left) won the 1964 Nobel Peace Prize for leading nonviolent civil rights marches.

Jessye Norman (1945–) is an opera singer. In her hometown of Augusta, the amphitheater and plaza overlooking the Savannah River have been named for her.

Flannery O'Connor (1925–1964) wrote about life in the South. She won the 1972 National Book Award for fiction.

Otis Redding (1941–1967) was a rhythm-and-blues singer. He began his career in Macon.

Little Richard (1932–) is a rock-and-roll singer and pianist with a wild, flashy style. He was born Richard Wayne Penniman.

Jackie Robinson (1919–1972) was the first African-American to play major-league baseball. He was named to the Baseball Hall of Fame in 1962.

Clarence Thomas (1948–) is a judge. In 1991, he became only the second African-American appointed to the U.S. Supreme Court.

Ted Turner (1938–) founded three cable television networks. They are the Turner Broadcasting System (TBS), Cable News Network (CNN), and Turner Network Television (TNT). Born in Ohio, Turner moved to Georgia as a child.

Alice Walker (1944–) is a poet and novelist. Her books include *The Color Purple* (1982).

Joanne Woodward (1930–) is an actress. Her movies include *The Three Faces of Eve* (1957).

Andrew Young (1932–) was the U.S. ambassador to the United Nations (1977–1979) and later served as mayor of Atlanta (1982–1989).

Want to Know More?

At the Library

Coleman, Brooke. *The Colony of Georgia.* New York: PowerKids Press, 2000.

Sibley, Celestine. *Christmas in Georgia.* Atlanta, Ga.: Peachtree Publishers, 1985.

Stechschulte, Pattie. *Georgia.* Danbury, Conn.: Children's Press, 2001.

Wills, Charles A. *A Historical Album of Georgia.* Brookfield, Conn.: Millbrook Press, 1996.

On the Web

The Georgia Historical Society
http://www.georgiahistory.com
To learn more about the history of Georgia

Georgia Net
http://www.state.ga.us/
For information on Georgia's history, government, economy, and land

Tourism in Georgia
http://www.georgia.org/tourism/
For a look at Georgia's events, outdoor activities, and heritage sites

Through the Mail

Georgia Department of Industry, Trade, and Tourism
285 Peachtree Center Avenue N.E.
Suites 1000 and 1100
Atlanta, GA 30303
For information on travel, interesting sights in Georgia, and Georgia's economy

On the Road

Atlanta History Center
130 West Paces Ferry Road N.W.
Atlanta, GA 30305
404/814-4000
To learn more about the history of Georgia

Georgia State Capitol
206 Washington Street
Atlanta, GA 30334
404/656-2844
To visit Georgia's capitol

Index

About the Author

Ann Heinrichs grew up in Fort Smith, Arkansas, and lives in Chicago. She is the author of more than eighty books for children and young adults on Asian, African, and U.S. history and culture. Ann has also written numerous newspaper, magazine, and encyclopedia articles. She is an award-winning martial artist, specializing in t'ai chi empty-hand and sword forms.

Ann has traveled widely throughout the United States, Africa, Asia, and the Middle East. In exploring each state for this series, she rediscovered the people, history, and resources that make this a great land, as well as the concerns we share with people around the world.